Long Cuts

J. O. Morgan lives in Scotland and has known Rocky, on whose life this book is based, for many years.

Praise for *Natural Mechanical*:

'Remarkable. A gem of a poem' – Simon Armitage

'*Natural Mechanical* is wonderful – a memoir written in language that is cannily involved with the ordinary miracles of childhood. By looking hard and exactly at particular things in a particular place, it speaks to everyone, everywhere.' – Andrew Motion

'So vivid it is clearer than prose. If those who never touch poetry tried a few pages of this, they might become converts.'
– Rosemary Goring, *Herald*

'It is not the slightest bit quaint or sentimental. It is a shower, a veritable downpour, of fine particulars in a single robust life . . . It is one vivid gathering sensation in skilfully calibrated language.'
– George Szirtes, *Poetry London*

'This arrestingly lovely memoir' – *Scotsman*

'*Natural Mechanical* is a higher achievement than Barry Hines' *A Kestrel for a Knave*, because it is more finely written . . . Rocky simply *is* and Morgan's achievement in bringing him to life with such respect and restraint is remarkable.' – Hannah Salt, *Magma*

'A literally fabulous achievement.' – *Times Literary Supplement*

LONG CUTS

J. O. Morgan

further wanderings in the life
of Iain Seoras Rockliffe

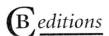 *editions*

First published in 2011
by CB editions
146 Percy Road London W12 9QL
www.cbeditions.com

Printed in England by Blissetts, London W3 8DH

ISBN 978–0–9567359–2–8

to
the only girl I ever really loved

Back for one month's recreational.
Back to Edinburgh.
Back for a night out with his biker pals. His bros.

Sat to one side of him
clutching their pints, their shots;
such a grip it's a wonder the glass doesn't crack,
sly shifting from empty to full
as they glug through the hours
sitting stiff through the hours
telling jokes, dirty jokes, and the rest.

Whilst Rocky, with his own drink,
his drink that is and is not quite a drink,
a cloudy pallid gently hissing drink,
strokes his thumb against the glass
to let the moisture congregate into a drip,
to let the drip pick out its wayward path
over his skin, his knuckles' soft red hairs,
to linger at the lowest point,
to drip, and be forgotten.

Till his pals run out of jokes
and start on him, for a while, at least.

What's it to be then, Rocky?
Land air or sea now, Rocky?
How come you never buy a round, Rocky?
Can you count the cunts on two hands yet, Rocky?
Can you speak to us in Japanese, Rocky?
Can you fix our mam's new dryer, Rocky?
Give us one of your tales, Rocky.
Give us a lift in your car, Rocky.
Give us a laugh, Rocky.
You're so full of shite, Rocky.

He takes it in good humour,
has learnt it's best to shut his hole;
a slit of smile to pucker up his face.

Whilst on his other side,
a flock of dolly birds who put away
as much drink as the men can manage,
though they go about it quietly,
of moments turn their whispers Rocky's way.

Is it not time you settled down, Rocky?
What about your apprenticeship, Rocky?
Did you ever see a thing the whole way through, Rocky?
Will you stop with all this gallivanting, Rocky?
Will you be good to her, Rocky?
Will you stick by her, Rocky?
Take us for a ride of your bike, Rocky.
Take us home with you, Rocky.
One by one, Rocky.

And, having said their piece, they turn their backs.

So Rocky downs his ginger beer,
its spice to sting his throat, to warm his gut,
wonders what the fuss is all about,
then checks his watch, counts to three,
takes a breath, holds it, stands

   That's me away.

and he is gone.

Dismissing thought on thought as he tears
down the empty length of Princes Street:

In truth who really cares
where he has been or what he's done.
The city is world enough for anyone.
Why ever leave?

Still grey shapes of suited men, seated
round one end of a long dark table
in a high wide-windowed office
overlooking downtown Perth,

Australia.

The air inside the room suffused
with particles of smoke slow lifting
from the half-inch smoulder of cigars,
held static, angled out on bony fingers.

A solid silver ashtray sliding its blue-felt base
over polished wood, pushed silently
from figure to figure, six large white pearls
rocking, huddled in its shallow dimple.

We need to locate where they're coming from.

The pearls are perfect, any eye
would note their fineness, held up
to strong sunlight, how their outer edge
disappears, a hazy circle hovering
in the gap between finger and thumb.

If it were merely one or two;
but a constant steady stream?
We suspect it's drugs related.

A small glossy map is produced, the sort
given free to tourists, triple-folded, displaying,
in entirety, the kidney-shaped continent.
It follows the pearls round the table.

Must be a port, or harbour, or some such.
Twenty reconnaissance flights; not spotted a thing.

A portion of the western edge, fatly ringed in red.
A two-hundred-mile stretch of uninhabited coast.
No major roadways. Mountain. Scrubland. Dust.

The council can't be seen to intervene.
Let's stumble upon this gang as if by accident.
Ostensibly your boys will be on exercises.
Hot-survival, that kind of get-up.

A military official, leaning closer to the map.
Leans back, passes it along
for its next brief dusting of ash.

  I'll need two four-by-fours,
  for the initial rough terrain.
  Nothing too fancy. Hardy. Reliable.

The Australian desert, stony flatlands,
bands of gritty brown, fading backward
to the sudden sharp grey cut-out of hills.
Beneath a white haze: two stationary jeeps.

  A few trackers would be useful. Native folk.
  Pick those accustomed to our western ways.

Figures milling round the jeeps.
Four in sandy fatigues, booted,
fanning themselves with their caps.
Four in jeans and red check shirts,
black-haired, dark-skinned, barefoot,
perched on the back of the jeeps,
stood on the roof, erect, still.

  The trucks no doubt will break down.
  No matter, I've a man in mind for that.

The bonnet of one of the trucks is up. Bent inside:
a stocky young man with short wavy hair.
A tracker stands behind him, silent,
watching every movement he makes.

A blown head-gasket. The young man strips it
using the four small spanners he has on him.
A short length of copper wire,
heated in the shade of the bonnet
with a gas lighter borrowed from the tracker,
passing the tip of stout orange flame
up and down the wire's thinness
till its pinkish sheen has turned a cherry red.
Quenched in an ounce of water, curled
into the gasket as it is put back together;
the tightening of parts to mould its shape.

The vehicles travelling side by side, kicking up dust;
a fine red cloud obscuring the way they have come.
Rocky, sat in the back with the trackers,
gripping the rim of the jeep as it bumps over stones,
squints into the unrelenting blast of sun-scorched air.

The jeeps are just to get them to the hills:

a massive ridge of stone, no warning slope,
no steady inclination, grown
sharply from the plain;
a ring of shady greens, of cooling waters,
of the call and flutter of bird shapes,
marking the transition from flat to sheer rock.

The trackers know the way up, set the path,
no time to dawdle, admire the view, up they all trudge,
with their minimal packs, their refilled canteens.

From the top one direction looks just as flat
and barren as the other; so down they all clamber,
through dry gullies, into shady trees, cooling waters.

The sun sets, the trackers stand, watching
as the soldiers set up camp, watching Rocky
going through his nightly rituals.

How he pisses in the sand around a hole
in which he's placed his metal cup, sets a plastic bag
over the wetted patch, pulled taut on sticks,
a pebble to indent the polythene.

The trackers watch, they wait, till he
gets up at dawn, picks one boot from one end
of the tent, the other from the other, where
he placed them, the night before.

Then to the plastic bag, its tentative scaffold,
deconstructed, gently, shaking the last few drips
of clear moisture into the partly filled cup, lifted
from its hole, the cup out of which he now drinks.

The trackers smile, showing their teeth,
saying nothing, turning to watch
the other men, sipping from canteens,
gingerly. They smile anew.

They walk beside Rocky through the day.
They walk on ahead, return to him,
show him their old maps: one side ordnance,
the other mosaiced with earthy colours.

See.

They point at the map.
They point to the ground at their feet.
The coloured grains of soil
from which they mix their paints.

See.

They point at the map, at the sky.

In their hands: the dotted symbol of a bird.
Far above: the cross of an eagle circling.

The trackers know what is required.
They have a good idea of where to go.
They head for the coast, and, reaching it,
follow it northwards, step by step.

A world divided, split upon the line they follow.
One side brown and flat and still.
The other sun-spangled, rippling, blue.

They walk. They eat. They sleep. They walk.

See.

Ahead,
a cluster of long black boulders.
On the map: more shades of brown
and doodled pointillistic fish
where ocean should be.

See. See.

Till the boulders resolve
into the upturned hulls of boats.
Supported on thick stilts.
Black with bitumen and weeds.

Till what seemed as heat waves
blurring the base of rocks
condenses into sticks of people
milling between the boats,
a steady line of traffic
down to the shore and back.

   Here.

Said with assurance, with nodding heads.
As though they had forever known its whereabouts;
declining to say, insisting it be shown.

Entering the settlement unhindered, observed
by women nursing children in the shadow of their homes,
by men who pause from perfecting their pearling seeds.

Young girls rise out of the lapping ocean edge,
bare-breasted, golden-skinned, short wet black hair,
a girdle round their waists supporting net and knife.

Small people, busy people,
not local: Vietnamese.

The old steamer on which they arrived,
since stripped, plundered,
divided into houses,
covered over, fixed in place,
no thought to any need of leaving.

Briefly assessing the situation, the soldiers
unpack their radio equipment,
send out coordinates;
a short report to end the mystery.

Two quiet hours pass beside the sea,
the guests being treated to fried octopus,
to gunpowder tea, unfolded from crepe paper;

before relief is helicoptered in
along with a photographer,
a journalist on the hop;
cans of fuel, of water,
fresh provisions, luxuries.

A short bout of activity,
information gathering,
and they are ready to be off,
back inside their helicopter,
on and up and away.

Though Rocky is left with the pearl farmers,
and the trackers waive a free lift home,
continue their northward stroll along the coast,
updating their maps as they go.

> *The influx of pearls still constitutes an economic problem.*
> *Though better than if it had all been connected to drugs.*

Rocky, trying to communicate with the Vietnamese,
taking walks along the shore with one of the elders,
cutting shapes into sand to serve instead of words.

How long will you leave your boy out with them?

Finding and fixing their single generator, not broken,
just old; stripping and cleaning it, making it new.

  He's a strange one. He likes this sort of thing.
  We sail in two weeks. I'll send for him then.

Sat by the men at their oyster surgeries,
how carefully the creature is sedated, becalmed,
as hand-ground spheres of shell are eased
into its pinkish folds.

  In-breeding is bound to be an issue after so long.
  We've others of their type. We'll fly them out, to mix.
  It's a lucrative trade. Can't see them complaining.

A trio of diving girls, urging him
to come and swim with them, provide
an old green oval-windowed mask,
its salt-bleached skin of withered silicone
tight-sucking to his face.

Following lengths of knotted rope
descending plumb into the gloom,
a girl on each arm to tug him deeper,
his mask gone misty, tunnelled vision,
all he can see through a penny-wide hole:
a pale pair of legs working the press of water.

His lungs begin to ache, unwilled
convulsions in his diaphragm,
he squirms; they let him go.

And as he rises limply, allowing the ocean
to squeeze him skyward, he sees them still,
faint fish-like shadows, pushing
ever down into the thickening blue.

In an Edinburgh backstreet
the office of an engineering firm.

A dusty closed-off corner
of split shelves and cracked walls
kept tidy if not clean by the gaffer
sat behind his cast iron desk.

This won't take long.

Spying through yellowed glass
into the waiting room, where a lad
devoid of education idles in his seat
in hope of easy work for little pay.

Can't be more than fifteen,
despite what he may tell me.

Taking a broom to lay across the floor
one step inside the doorway, standing back,
pretending to get on with paperwork,
as offhandedly he calls for the boy,

who comes in
sees the broom
puts it away.

Who gave you permission
to touch what isn't yours?

As the boy sits down,
his no-nonsense demeanour,
eyes in a permanent sun-bright wince,
marking every move the gaffer makes.

I'll put it back if you'd prefer,
though someone's sure to fall on their arse.

Taken on a tour of the workshop,
between heavy machines and heavy labourers,

This place gets messy quickly.
You'll work faster to keep the dirt in check.
Plus helping out wherever else you can.

the waver of chains, of belts reaching up to the rafters,
the dark and the dust, the glow from furnaces.

Four years for a fitter's apprenticeship.
And that's only if you show promise.

But the boy is not listening,
has already begun to pass
through the sudden shifts in heat
to clear away the concentrated grime
collected round the workmen's feet.

A wolf, in white, setting his splay of paws
to the bootprints cut in the snow, left
by men he's been tracking for days.
Never far back yet never too close.

Sniffing at the traps they've set,
not meant for him; a hare, just as white,
warm within a taut grass snare, which
he takes, grateful for the courtesy.

Come night, he lies without the ring of light
flickered through the forest from their fire,
curled in a snowhole, beneath a clear sky;
the same bright stars to shine on him as them.

Naught left of their camp come the morning, except
the single crooked remnant of a burned-out match,
its stub of white wood coated thinly with wax;
the latent warmth of a fire brushed over with snow.

Having to quicken his lope now they've taken to skis.
One set of smooth pressed tracks uneven,
signs of an accentuated limp, the lag
of the lame, succumbing to strain as to cold.

Regaining the shelter of mountain forests
the wolf strays from their trail, distracted
by the sense of having been here before,
how the path has looped round on itself.

Fresh cracked ice, centring a static pool.
A single maple leaf floated in the hole.
A silver pin resting at the leaf's middle.
The wolf's head lifts. He is watched.

Cresting a ridge between two pines
a white-clad figure, belly to the snow;
not much to see of him but the small black hollow
of the rifle's muzzle, the glass eye of the scope.

The wolf gazing, unmoving, till the rifleman
lifts his own line of sight from the scope;
the long yellow glare of the slim white wolf
set against the shadowed indent of his squint.

Till the curve of a wood-stump, bearded with lichen,
explodes beside the calm startle of wolf;
a rain of wet splinters puncturing snow, amidst which
he turns about, retracing the way he has come.

Weekly wages for a benchhand, sweeper-upper, monkey-boy:
two pounds, nineteen shillings, nine and a half pence.
He's good at saving it, good at using it too.

A little goes on cigarettes, not much, just short of a florin
for five Senior Service, tipped, to last him
from Monday to Friday. It's mostly for show.

Catching the bus into town from his home in the suburbs
to go to the picture-house; goes there alone, can't see much
for the smoke-haze, enhancing the sense of a world not his own.

At the ice-rink in Princes Street Gardens, in winter;
the wool-padded giggles of girls slipping over, he brakes,
stands them up, sets them going, then skates off himself.

Not permitted to linger at home, but expected to be back
in time for his duties, to ready the table for dinner, to set up
the coal fire each night; a heavy hand to welcome him if late.

Spooling through the weekends on a bus, a day-long ticket,
terminus to terminus, a city etched through juddered glass,
transports his thought away; never going far enough.

Called into the office
where the gaffer and a man in tweed
pore over papers spread upon the desk.

> *This man's a surgeon; from the hospital.*
> *He wants us to make him an object, like this.*
> *See if we've anything that could be modified.*

Rough sketches, detailed annotations.
A scribble of words, meaning nothing to Rocky,
except for the shape of the thing.
Some sort of ball and socket joint
to fit inside a reconstructed limb.

They say they'll let him know.
The surgeon leaves, taking his diagrams.
The gaffer, catching Rocky's arm
before he goes too.

> *Don't let it interfere with your duties.*
> *It can't be helped if we can't help him.*

Called by the senior caster
who hands him a slip of paper.

Need a pattern for this valve cluster.
And we're running low on brass.

Rocky's glance at the code he's been given.
Shinning up ropes to the pattern shelves,
to the gloom of the rafters,
forty feet above the workshop floor.

Matching the shapes on the slip with those on the box.
Balancing the wooden sculpture on his head as he descends.

Out in the backyard, donning leather gauntlets,
he sorts through the jagged tangle of metals,
drags back a box of twisted bits of brass
to add to the furnace; left within to melt.

Called by the machinist
turning a ship's plug between his fingers.

We need to make a hundred and fifty of these.
Take note on how I cut the first.

Though he makes no notes, only watches
as the diamond tool-tip bites the spinning brass,
as filigreed spirals of swarf peel hot into the trough,
then goes to work on setting up the capstan lathe
to copy the process with callipered precision.

Preparing to go on call-out
to install a printing press.

Just need to test it one last time.
Make up a sentence, any sentence, for the block.

Directed to a tray of fine lead type.
The tumble of backward lettering.
Dizzying silver-faced twists of solid sound,
staying silent for him,
withholding comprehensibility.

Just one sentence, Rocky.
Just a line, a single recognisable word.

Summoned to the front office.
The gaffer, arms folded, considers him.

I can offer you apprenticeship as a fitter.
Plenty of work for a fitter. Variety too.

Rocky thinks for a moment. Thanks him.
Then explains why he must decline.

A fitter fits the parts he buys.
An engineer makes the parts he needs.

Followed by the gaffer's explanation,
how it's not as simple as that,
how each skill must be practiced in turn.

Which, for what you want, adds up to seven years.
You're going to stick around for all that?

Closing up the workshop for the day.
Sweeping out water
thrown down to calm the dust,
to thin the fumes,
to soften the furnace's breath.

Rocky, on his way home, drops into the hospital,
leaves a package with the girl at reception,
describing in detail the man it's for.

The girl's nervous smile set against
Rocky's determined instructions.

> *I know who you mean. He's a surgeon.*
> *But you can't leave this here unopened.*

So the package is unwrapped and the girl
lifts out the small articulated object,
made of brass, lightweight, perfectly smooth.

She wiggles it before her eye.
It looks harmless enough.
She asks what it's for.

> *I don't know. Some sort of joint.*
> *He asked for it to be made. So I made it.*

Thick milk-misted ice, flat-topped, close
beside the shallow curve of a grey steel wall.

The wall's steady vibration,
a deep reverberant hum.
The echoed whistles of the ice
sped in all directions.

A dark gap between two solids.
Its unseen suck of water.

The gap begins to close, narrows
to a crack, a divisional split.
The wall drifting towards the ice.
The ice butting up against the wall.

They rub.

The metal moans.
The ice howls.
Briefly.

They move apart.

Yellow electric light upon ice and wall.
Booted feet. A man in padded orange overalls.
He carries a large red hand-drill.
A massive screw, four feet long, three inches
between the blades of its deep-grooved thread.

A few paces from the wall, the man
stabs the tip of the drill into the ice,
centring the patch of yellow light.

Gloved hands, powerful arms,
twisting the crossbar, drilling in.
The spiral's sharp edge biting
down into the ice.
A froth of fine white particles
spilling up, out of the hole.

Stopping as the crossbar reaches
the level of his shins, with him
now crouched beside it,
reverses the twist, an easy
one-fingered spin upwards.

Compacted ice stuck between its teeth
falling away as the drill rises.

The man,
supporting the drill in the crook of one elbow,
fishes in the pockets of his overalls, extracts
a long thin stick of gelignite
clothed in dull red paper,
a nine-inch dangle of safety-fuse
the tip of which he lights,
before dropping the jelly-stick into the ice,
and walking away.

The explosion: funnelling out of the hole.

A jet of ice and water, shot straight upward
high into the smoky grey sky.

The boom: happening everywhere at once,
travelled through the expanse of ice
undiminished, to be absorbed into
the dark bordering of forest.

A great white lake.
A great grey boat.
The failing light of day.
The distant drone of engines.

Put into reverse, the ship backs up, shortly,
through a broken trail of ice, re-forming, re-broken,
before driving forward, hard into the skin of the lake,
with a sound to equal that of the exploding gelignite,
as the ice fractures, the split forming faster than sound,
the sonic boom of its leading edge
ripped through the watery dark beneath.

A few more yards of progress.

The ship idles, begins to drift backwards.
Its painted steel side rubbing against the ice.

A sea-ship trapped in fresh water,
its lifeboats lowered onto the frozen lake,
their generators powering strong electric lamps,
as men in orange overalls move over the solid white,
twisting thin holes beside the bow,
as the daylight fades,
to the booming of the fractured ice,
to the laboured whine of engines.

The Post Office being
the only bank to open at weekends,
and only then till half twelve,
come Saturday morning it fills quick
with a zigzag of labourers,
Rocky amongst them
as one of the working men.

Of less importance today to pay in
the little that remains of last week's wage
than to check on his accumulated wealth,
to ask the big bespectacled lady behind
the glass to write the figure down.

After which it's across to Lothian Road,
to meander through the showrooms for the bikes,
noting current prices, getting his research up to date.

He is good with numbers, they make more sense to him,
each simply squiggled shape to represent
a standard comprehensible unit of measure.

Beside the prices he draws the words
for model and make, visually stencilling
the pattern of their name from fuel tank to paper,
colours from paper tags hung from their handles.

Passing the curve of his palm around, untouching,
the lines of a Norton Commando Fastback;
a motorised angel, balancing its stainless temperament.

Though no insurance company would risk
a payout to some power-hungry youth
newly straddling anything over 250cc,
which leaves

FRANCIS BARNETT PLOVER	(TEAL)	– £94
JAMES CADET	(KHAKI)	– £112
BSA BANTAM	(BOTTLE)	– £150
TRIUMPH TIGERCUB	(SCARLET)	– £168

Pristine machines, hard-angled skeletons
stretching their frames low between thin black wheels,
the small silver lumps of engine, flat-ribbed hives,
floated in the central gap, pipes leading down and back.

All over-glossed with wax, all over-oiled,
broad sheets of yesterday's news spread beneath
to catch the gold-rimmed black drips seeping
from the cut cork bung of their gaskets.

Near-late home for the evening meal
the tension in the air is palpable, with nothing said
as he sets up the dinner table, saying nothing;
waiting through potted beef, pale sponge pudding,
waiting for his father to be filled.

The little big man, at the table end, sat stiff-muscled,
chin tucked into his neck, both eyes on his wife,
in watching the boy draw a notebook from his pocket.

Father, if it's okay, I'd like your advice.

Leafing to the page not looking up
at his father not moving in his seat.

I've been doing the calculations myself.
I've been round the shops to see which bike's the best.
I've saved up forty-five pounds, five shillings, and tuppence.
It's not enough alone, but if I bought on the never-never

Though he has been sitting tight, the blow
from his father's hand comes so hard, so fast,
it knocks him from his chair onto the floor;
too slow to gather up notebook and pencil,
his father's grip around his wrist,
jerking him half upright, jabbing
the thick finger of his other hand
towards the figure busily ignoring from the kitchen.

That woman has never once got me into debt.
Neither will you.

At which he lets go, gets up, leaves the room,
comes back a few minutes later with his copy
of the Edinburgh Evening News, opens it
flat upon the table, straight
to the eighty-second column,
where the bikes are often to be found.

And they find one,
a BSA Bantam in blue,
175cc, within his means,
so they phone the number
and are told it's still available,
are told there's been a lot of interest,
are told: if they can come round,
this very day, this very hour.

Rocky pays the bus fare for them both,
sits eager on the top deck at the front,
while his father, wrapped in a thick black mac,
gazes fixedly out the window to one side.

The address is for the warden's cottage
at the Pollock Halls of residence, and though
they find the student complex easily enough
they can't find the cottage; the bright-garbed
girls leant out of windows, smoking, being
of little use in locating its whereabouts; as Rocky
begs for their assistance, they only shake
their long-haired heads, and duck back out of sight.

It took half an hour to get there from Liberton,
half an hour more of unsuccessful wandering,
with Rocky growing ever more frantic,
with his father feeling they ought to get back home,
till he spies not the bike, nor the cottage, but
a long black glossy tarpaulin, at once knowing
the bulge of skinny shape it drapes.

Started up for them, Mr Rockcliffe Sr. sets
his expertise to work in giving the machine
the once-over, ear to the engine's wavered grumble,
using the stand as pivot to lift the back wheel,
to squeeze the throttle, watching it spin, then,
at the gentlest pressure on the brakes, stop dead.

Satisfied, he heads in with the warden
to negotiate a price, leaving the bike ticking over,
leaving the boy (once his father has gone)
to perform his own checks, not touching,
stood one pace away, eyes closed, studying its sound,
the piston cough, the hiccup, drop in pitch, in power;
nothing he can't mend, or make, himself; is satisfied.

Unlicensed, as yet, he waits for the bus,
having watched the speck of his bike, of his father,
shrinking down the slope of Dalkeith Road, its buzz
receding, to join the white hiss of common traffic.

The sky above the city turns grey, a smooth
velvety slate, while the low evening sunlight
streams yellow through the space beneath,
glows gold the white-harled walls of houses,
the thickness of sky to descend as gilded rain.

Rain drums the laminated calico,
an old stiff tablecloth Rocky has spread
over the bike and over himself, perched
knees up on the backdoor step,
polishing the paintwork of his bike,
his BSA Bantam, in blue.

Though to him it is more than mere blue,
it is midnight, abyssal, leviathan, it is
the deep choppy waters of lochans amidst
moorland on the isle where he grew up.

His father's bike is never to be touched;
not used these days so much, stays covered
in the shed, as Rocky sidles past to reach
for the petrol tin; careful to re-trail cobwebs
over the gap left on the shelf at its taking.

Half a mile to the nearest set of pumps is nothing
to his steady stride, there and back in fifteen minutes;
transferring his gallon of fuel to his teardrop tank.

The tin back on the shelf, re-cobwebbed,
as he tightens the RAF goggles over his nose,
too big, their leather-trimmed windows
unfitting to his face, will do well enough,
as he kicks up the bike,
and is gone.

His tinkering restricted to the lunch hour,
though the gaffer does not mind much to see him
nosing through the high-grade scrap out back,
taking some part from his pocket he took from his bike,
seeking to match the metal if not the shape,
much easier to alter than to manufacture new;
so long as it does not interfere with his duties,
so long as he pays for the metal he uses.

The gaffer doesn't mind because come lunchtime
the boy's other role moves to the fore, as the men
crowd round to give him their orders, and Rocky
notes it all down in his pocket-book, orders
for pie, for bridies, for dense chunks of cake,
plus those items that to him seem luxurious:
the bottles of Coke, bags of crisps, coffee cartons.
He notes it all down, takes their money, goes off,
returning with one big lot for them to divide,
provides receipts, with never a half-penny lost.

Except the gaffer knows how the boy can't write,
managing one day to sneak a look at that pocket-book
whilst Rocky is busy away from his corner of workbench.
No words on any pages, only symbols; basic shapes
to start off with, circles, triangles, squares, though
as the pages turn the symbols develop, their shapes
distort, break apart, marks are added, floating
embellishments, dotted denotations, of flavour, filling,
white bread or brown, a tally beside each for each day,
no names, which is why the food arrives in one big lot.

Once the lunch has been deposited he goes back
to his tinkering, working throughout the hour,
machining fresh engine parts, never lacking
for something to do; with this going on
for so many weeks, the gaffer wonders
just how many bikes the boy owns,
later learning that requests come frequently
from other bike owners; a problem;
a business within a business?
The authorities wouldn't like that.

It's fine, they never pay me for the work.
They don't? All the more reason for you to stop.

Just because he's out on the town.
Just because he's loitering.
Just because his pals look like
they're up to no good.

Just because he happens to be passing
and spies Rocky standing there,
his father stops
and gives him a thrashing;
his belt to the boy's back.

The onlookers semi-scatter
but half-won't half-can't go far.

And she sees him too; she's there:
the one he'll someday fall in love with.
She'll recall he didn't cry out,
hardly even cowered, took each hit,
never saying a word,
heading for his bike and home.

She'll remember it all
though she'll not mention it.
The sting of each blow.
The clink of the buckle.

The next cabin along from his belongs to Jojo: a man from
  the Philippines; delicately framed; not tall.

He is teaching Rocky aspects of his language, which Rocky
  picks up quick, so long as it is aurally taught.

Jojo is known for dressing up in women's clothing, just for
  the spectacle, and because he has the figure for it.

So when the ship is in port, and two pairs of bright stilettos
  sit neatly outside his door, no one can say for sure whom
  they belong to.

A refuelling tug, alongside the hard blank curve of the hull,
  the tip of its fat black hose snug within the big ship's
  spacious tanks.

Rocky knocks at Jojo's door; it's one thing to have a woman
  on board while the ship is docked, quite another while
  they're moving.

It is evening. Jojo wanders the deck in a red summer dress, a
  wide straw hat; the shorewind sucking the red silk to his
  slender thighs.

One hand on the brim of his bonnet, the other splayed over
  his chest, he leans from the railings, calls to the tug-men,
  in their dialect.

They look up. They smile, laugh, whistle, nod. Matters
  discussed, agreements made. Jojo slinks back from the
  boat's high edge.

Some time later, the same red dress, the same straw bonnet,
  the same dark complexion beneath, stepping nervously up
  to the railings.

A thin-runged wooden ladder, extended upward from the
  tug, poked between the narrow bars, slipping on the
  smooth painted lip.

The red dress descending slowly the bend of the bridge, to
  cooing from the tug-men, shoes dangled on fingertips,
  skirt hem fluttering.

Safely aboard, safely stowed below, the ladder collapsed, the
  fat black hose, uncoupled, retracted, the tug swings away.

Leant against the ship's railings, Jojo and Rocky, watching
  the tug chug through black water, through yellow
  harbour lights.

Then back below decks, to get the engines up to speed, to
  head out for a new unknown destination, for a dress of
  some different colour.

His father's house: his father's rule.

At eighteen years, he leaves.
He buys a caravan, stationed out at Roslin.

The ground rent is minimal. His caravan has a bath.
He keeps all of its small interior obsessively clean.
Bedsheets changed weekly; washed within; hung without.
He is accomplished at using the stove;
his little windows are often fogged of an evening.

When coaxed to come into the city at night
he finds it easier these days to decline.
He can stay at home all weekend if he wants,
tending his small square of grass, his dwarf gorse,
sat out in the sun, beneath the heavy flap of the washing line.

Though the invites persist, are embellished,
how he's missed, how it's not the same when he's not there,
how he's always good for a laugh, how there's sure
to be more girls if he's around.

It's true enough, but once out the aim is changed,
in trying to get him to chip in with the drinks.
What they earn in the week sluiced down their throats,
or the throats of girls who choose to tag along;
not yet aware of their need for mothering,
not yet familiar with the dial of a washing machine.

One girl asks him why he doesn't drink, whether
it's a religious thing; a quiet comely girl who sits
close by him all evening. Her name is Islay.

He answers simply how it makes him sick, the alcohol,
of how the slightest sip gets thrown back up,
how his father was ever the same, and how
his mother won't touch it, her dumbed obedience.

When the group splits at midnight, some stumbling
for the bus, some lifting skirts down unlit lanes,
Islay stays with him. When he gets to where
he's parked his bike, she is still there.

It's awkward, given the bike is not fitted for passengers.
She has to sit on his lap. Her knees tight to the tank,
his knees squeezing to hold her in place.
The fat double spring of the seat creaking under the load.

The caravan is cold when they arrive.
He brews a pot of tea. She takes off her top.
He says he's never had a guest before. She doesn't mind.
He apologises a lot. She tells him not to.

It seems to take an age,
is more tiring than he expected
without really getting anywhere in the end.

Once through
she gathers her things
and goes to run a bath.

Rocky, hands shaking, shuts the caravan door
without making a sound, freewheels his bike
partway down the track, before starting it
and riding off alone into the night.

Thin black rubber ripping itself to the road.

The sweat soaked into his clothes blow-dried
by the speed of air passing around him.
The headlamp glowing its wide yellow ring
down the tunnel of trees arced overhead.

He doesn't know where he's going, just goes,
through Penicuik, to Peebles, and beyond.
Any thought of returning met by the image
of her lying nude in his bath, so at ease,
wet-haired, her little breasts bobbing
up through the soap-scummed water.

He stays out all night,
his back to his bike;
pictures her curled
alone beneath his sheets.

A packet of biscuits bought cheap
from a garage for breakfast;
and her in his gown, making toast,
browsing old newspapers.

Early afternoon when he returns
to perfect tidiness; the bed made up,
the bath rinsed out, a note
left corner-tucked beneath the kettle,
twenty lines long, he follows
the elegant swirl of her script
with patience, unsmiling,
the words themselves
to remain undecipherable.

Back out on request.

Three weeks into his three-month leave
he phones his Colonel from a callbox,
explains how he can't stand being home
with nothing much round here for him to do.

We've a boat docked at Vancouver.
Not due to move out till the weekend.
Plenty of time to get you on board.

From the military strip at which he lands
he takes a taxi to the city.
They've pre-booked him at a hotel,
all paid in advance.

The Canadian girl at reception
shows him to his room;
he doesn't want to put her to the trouble,
she assures him she's not busy.

The room is small and cold but not damp.
The wallpaper: vertical burgundy stripes over beige.
There is a tall wardrobe in one corner,
a fitted wash-hand basin in another.
The single bed is narrow and low.
The sheets are cream.
There is nothing else.

I hope all is to your satisfaction.
Let me know if there's anything more that you want.

And she goes.

His frost-fringed window faces west
but he can't see the sea from here,
only the walls of buildings opposite,
the squares of yellow light,
the motions of people within.

Rising early for breakfast
he's the only one there to be served;
the restaurant as extension to the bar.

The maple-syrup provided with his pancakes
presented in a small ceramic dish;
it is warm and dark brown;
once he's finished his bacon and scrambled egg,
he drinks the thick liquid at a gulp.

The ship is in dock.
The engines are off but still it vibrates in the water.
Always much work to be done when at rest.

Uniformed men move over the studded deck.
Rocky strolls the harbour in dark green cords
and padded donkey jacket, they wouldn't know him
as one of their own, even without the fur-lined cap;
though the boots are a giveaway.

Frequenting a club called The Old Mariner,
popular with all sorts of sea-faring folk,
popular with anyone happening to drop by,
a quiet grey-lit place with painted wood floors,
with fat lengths of rope knotted over the fire,
a stuffed, glazed marlin mounted behind the bar.

He watches two staff-members carry a man,
a North-American Indian, with vomit on his twill shirt,
out of the club, into the bright of the street,
leaving him there, acquiescent, in a daze,
gone semi-paralytic, rubber-legged,
apparently from too much booze.

Another Indian, sat beside Rocky,
watching as he watches,
turning away as the door swings to,
the sad folds of his too-old face
dipping forward over his ice-cream soda,
curling his wiry black hair behind one ear.

He should know better.
We red-men can't digest it.
The younger ones: a little:
a small light beer, no more.

He takes a long sip of his soda,
licks a film of vanilla from his lips.

But once you have become of-the-city
there is no going back to the land of one's birth;
it is changed, you are changed,
you are neither one man nor another.

The long flat shape of his hand
passing sideways, cuts the air, shortly.

There is nothing can be done.
You may try to fit in.
You will remain outside, unsettled.

Rocky,
strolling up the walkway to the ship,
uniformed in black, topped neatly
with a powder-blue beret.

All he needs to get by, squashed
into the kit-bag slung at his hip;
showing his papers to the sentry,
and on.

Though never part of their card-schools, their cliques,
he still hangs about while they play.

He can join in whenever he wants.
We'll teach him. We'll let him deal.
He only ever seems to want to watch.

Wondering just how he ended up here.
Cadet Club was good for a while;
this long-term barrack life
never part of the plan.

It'll get you off the street corners at weekends.
Get some discipline into that stupid head.
Teach you to fire a rifle, to be a man.

The square bashing: no worse than at home.
The sergeant's bark: his father on an average day.
Reacts by not reacting. Gets on. Does.

A brand new pair of marching boots,
and he goes and pisses in them,
first thing in the morning, strong stuff,
left them brim-filled, stank out the mess.

Coming back from their four-mile run, limping
on toe-tips with bloodied heels, whilst he
slips off the softened leather, lies back
in perfect comfort on his bunk.

Any vehicle breakdown, he'll fix it, like that.
A skill to surpass mere mechanics.
I put in a word. Got him into the engineers.
At junior rank, on account of his poor spelling.

Hanging up his uniform, cleaned and brushed,
from the roof-rail inside his caravan.
Sitting back in vest and pants, cup of tea
on his lap, staring at the thick material,
at the bright polished brass of the buttons,
the thin purple line round the wrist of each sleeve.

She spies him as he comes into the bar,
separated from the others already here, snug
in his bright orange overalls, slinking
to a dark corner, to remain unnoticed.

He enters with stealth for fear of still stinking,
sits apart from his fellow men, orders root beer,
the only thing he feels he could keep down;
present, yet feeling it's best to be left alone.

She walks with him through the snow, he is
attentive, barely speaks, lets her set the pace,
his arm hugged in the hook of hers,
walking beneath a silent star-bright sky.

He has to move with baby steps
because his arse-hole is still sore, holding
tight to her as she clings to him, his muscles
taut, lest one escapes, with her so close.

Her parents, watching TV in the kitchen,
getting up, welcoming him to their home,
offer him dinner, drink, are impressed,
his abashed politeness, his soft declining.

The ache in his guts,
a nausea welling in his throat,
his tender skin, the flush in his cheeks,
the meekness of his voice when it comes out.

She leads him to her room, starts
to undress him, he protests, though weakly,
letting her peel away the padded orange,
lets her discover him knickerless beneath.

Explaining how hot it gets in the engine room,
(*of how the curry they dared him eat was hotter*)
how they must drink copious quantities of water,
(*on leaving the ship, the crunching of snow as his mask*)

a gallon of orange juice a day, salt tablets,
(*till, pushing one too hard, what the curry has become comes too*)
all that drink turned into perpetual perspiration,
(*dropping behind his crew-mates to clean himself up*)

with a necessity to maximise airflow
(*wiping bared skin with sphagnum moss, with snow*)
knickers are a hindrance, are soon soaked through
(*the offending garment discarded, buried under leaf mulch*).

Her curiosity assuaged, she strips,
and as they get down to it ponders the mix
of his bear-like strength, his mouse-like tenderness,
of how long his ship intends to stay in port.

With him too acutely aware of her parents
sat in the next room, watching TV,
and how she must never learn of his disgrace,
forever after knickerless for her.

He has washed, shaved, combed his hair,
put on clean white overalls, made his way
to the mid-ship, to Neptune's Lounge.

Here they serve the same as Pig's Bar, aft,
but without the permeating stench of sweat;
not a place to grab a snack, but to
relax, to close one's eyes for a time,
be easy-carried by the steady ploughing
of fifty thousand tons of floated steel, with
no thought to when the next shift begins.

 And they say a pig cannot sweat.
 I'm sure you boys more than make up for the lack.

Rocky, the slow lifting of his lids, to see
an officer, in whites of a different sort,
banded with gold, third rung down from the top,
slump into the opposite seat, tossing his peaked
white cap onto the table between them.

He says nothing in return, knows better,
knows it would get him nowhere to protest,
knows it's what the officer is waiting for:
a little confrontation, to relieve the boredom.

Not the first time this particular
high-ranked, self-important speck
of seamanship has found his way
from control-room to incessant rankling.

 I'm sure you're very useful in a crisis.
 If something needs fixing you fix it.
 It's why we have the likes of you aboard.

Snapped fingers to attract the duty waiter
already heading his way, military trained,
as are all the personnel upon the boat.

Then again if there's nothing broken.
One wonders how you while away the hours.
While my lot are heaving this brute around the globe.

Nothing for it but to leave before the sniding escalates.
Before the physical temptation overwhelms him.

He has been told that if this happens again then
he must report it to his superior; not that he believes
complaining ever does much good, the duly noted
concern, the frown, written down, the promise
of a reprimand that's sure to make the situation worse.

Nonetheless he makes his way below decks,
towards the juddered inner workings of the ship,
the constant knocks, the heavy pulse
of air around his ears as he descends.

He stops. Upon a narrow skeleton of stairs.
Because, he knows, this is ridiculous.

Beside him, set into the metal wall, identical
to several others that he passed and gave
no thought to, is a small glass panel, framed
in thick red plastic, which he considers, briefly.

A toffee-hammer: plucked from its double clips.
A sideways flick: its pointed metal tip to break the glass.
An ease contrary to its effect: in pulling the lever within.

There is a moment
between the generators shutting off
and emergency lights buzzing on;
a moment just after
the telegraphs upstairs and down
both slip into neutral;
a moment following
the cease of fuel pumped through the system,
the screws, unspun, to hang heavy in the blue;
a fractional moment
when there is total calm,
a ship made silent,
pacified and pensive,
lightly buoyed upon
the mirror-weight of ocean
its bloat has moved aside.

Before
every alarm in every quarter of the ship
begins to wail.

Amidst the sudden increase in bodily traffic,
of men half-dressed or half-asleep
all of a dash for their posts to see what's up,
the Chief Engineer,
second only to God,
spies Rocky,
arms folded, leaning against the wall
beside the broken glass panel,
with his scrunched-up face,
his clean white overalls, combed hair,
slowly shaking his head as the Chief
steps nearer, as frantic bodies flow between,
as the Chief points his finger

I'll deal with you later.

and melds into the stream of busyness
with Rocky duly following.

No power to force it forward,
all air blown from the ballast tanks,
undirected, the massive boat begins to bump,
to line itself, drifting, with the waves,
to rock in mute subservience to the water.

The start-up procedure is fairly straightforward.

The air compressor builds up pressure in the primary tank.
The pressure in the tank is used to fire the first generator.
The first generator is used in turn to start the others.
The stopcocks must all be reset to allow the diesel to flow.
The engines must be fully primed with fuel before they go.
The system needing constant water-cooling to slow the heat.

Except, it's never so straightforward.

The air compressor must be primed by hand.
The pressure required by the tank is 100psi.
The tank is as large as an average living room.
The cooling pipes' exhaust has rotted through.

The twelve engineers and their chief see to the engines
and to the working of the compressors.

The remainder of the crew,
every one of them,
including the officers,
including the third-in-command,
who, unbeknownst to him, is the cause
of this self-imposed-emergency-waste-of-time,
form one long relay,
passing buckets of seawater,
drawn from high on deck,
carried man to man,
deep into the ship,
to keep the compressor from overheating,
in an engine-room with an ambient temperature,
hotter than that of a healthy human body.

None of them know about keeping their own fluids up.
None of them are provided with salt tablets.
Many end up in the hospital unit
once the day is through, suffering
from severe dehydration;
the third-in-command amongst them.

It takes three hours to reach full pressure,
to fire the gennies, to start the vibrations,
the thumpings, the spin of the screws.
By which time the ship has drifted,
carried by the oceanic currents,
several miles from its course.

I say we drop him at the next port.

The Captain, conferring with the Chief.

And I say he's highlighted a crucial concern.

The Chief, refusing to be swayed.

That the deck officers have no clue
as to what goes on at lower levels.

A couple of engineers, up on the bridge,
being shown how decisions get made,
poring over maps, intelligence, working
the telegraph, sending the signals down.

That one hand doesn't know
and neither does the other
what each gets up to.

Officers taken on tours of the engines,
taught to pump bilges, make water, oil,
how to read a signal when it comes,
what it entails to action the command.

And Rockcliffe?
Am I expected to shake his hand?

Rocky too, gets his stint up top,
as does the third-in-command, below,
swapping places for a day,
thought best to keep them separate.

The NUMBER ONE you gave him is enough.
He knows, just once more, and he's out.

❖

The empty-matchbox lightness of a kayak,
covered single-seater, dipping to his weight
as he slides neatly in, seals up the hole,
joins to its wobbled buoyancy, top heavy
with him stuck out of its top, untipping,
surging swanlike out across the lake.

Some months ago upon his first encounter
with these oblong egg-shells guised as boats,
his first foot in was all that he could manage
as the stiff-set bubble drifted, spread his stance,
then dropped him in the shallows as it rocked away,
knocking its hollow nose against those tethered beside.

Now he has mastered the delicate touch,
can roll himself under and up, fully righted,
can sink it, up-end it, unflood it
and flop back on board, re-inserting himself,
re-connected. Now he teaches others like him
not to step as he stepped. Not to fall.

So much for his prowess on water;
it is yet not his favourite.

His favourite
is carefully folding and rolling
his parachute into his pack, not so tight
it won't catch on the air when he jumps,
not so loose it won't slip from his pack
at the tug of the cord.

The Hercules cruising at 10,000 feet
in the thinness of blue over mountains,
releasing its dandelion spawn, its thin spray
of silk jellyfish, too weak to pilot
their floppy brown mantles, drift down,
drifting where the wind takes them,
over the mottlings of the valley,
the wriggles of river, the clusters of pine
the speed of their falling becoming apparent,
the closer they come to the ground.

Rocky, lodged in the arms of a tree, part way down
from the point of its top, the air round him
suffused with the scent of oils burst from branches
that broke as he was caught, as he holds
what remains of his ankle, lest it comes loose
altogether, to topple, bouncing, to the forest floor,
where his blood is already headed, the smooth
blue-grey bones of his lower left leg
poked through the rip in his jumpsuit,
the sag of his parachute smeared like a skin
of hot milk on the skyward face of forest,
the only signal of his whereabouts.

At the military hospital, Perth,
the separate parts of his leg
matched, stitched together, held fast
with plates of stainless steel, a scaffold of pins
drilled into the bone, wrapped in flesh,
the blunted ends sat stiff beyond his skin.
The first plaster cast goes to the top of his thigh;
with a kilt on it doesn't much matter,
the thick oblong of white against the tartan's
hunting colours: browns, greys, thin bands of lilac.

The Colonel, having pulled some strings, taking him
to tour the inner decks of a new commission.
The cast now no more than a dirty white boot
clicking on the hard black floor of the hold,
the world-space belly of the ship, mostly empty
but for three dinky tanks, shy in the far dark corner,
their cloth-draped nozzles brittled by the vastness.

The generators in the engine room: as big as a bus,
as two busses, as a bus beside a bus with more roped on top.
In one: enough power produced to light a small town.
The ship has three. Rocky, stood before a panel
of 200 separate gauges, their needles at zero, for now,
as the Colonel pats his shoulder, and hands him the key.

Drifting in with the dawn
soft on six o'clock,
the hook gets dropped.
They hear it from within their deep chamber,
above the din of the engine's stand-by vibe:
the rasp of the ten ton chain through its hole;
the silence of a two-storey anchor, breaking the water.

And as it thumps into the sea-bed,
its chain, gone taut, tugs the boat to full-stop,
and Rocky's relief appears as his shift ends,
so, downing the dregs of his juice
he heads up top, to see where he'll come out.

Hot fog on deck.
Grey mist over soupy water;
glowed by the low sun;
making each particle sticky
with light and heat.

A floating village, shanty town,
chugging into visibility,
slipping forward over murky green,
a raft of box-crate houses, corrugated roofs;
the steam puffed from their engines thickens the mist,
a jumble of voices devoid of hard edges,
elongated vowels, emoting, calling, bird-like,
piloting their wooden jetty up beside the ship.

His guess is for Shanghai.
He's told it's Hong Kong.
Not far wrong, but too tired
to stay and watch.

His corridor overfluoresced with electric light,
unwincing into the gloom of his private oven,
the air-con having packed up in the night,
so splays himself, stripped naked,
sweating into the dip of his bunk.

Shuffled footsteps in the corridor.
Subdued chatter mixed with semi-sleep.

His door swings open.
His hand held up to the glare.

You want girl?

A girl-shaped figure distorted by the light,
wavered through the gaps between fingers.

I'm very tired.

The figure doesn't move.
Staring at him where he lies.

Second engineer. He send me. You want?

He hasn't moved either.
More light coming in than he knows.

I really couldn't, but thank you.

She goes.
The sound of her pattering away.
He has to close the door himself.

Near falling again into sleep he hears
the patter re-growing, now doubled,
stopped outside, more chatter, faster,
the opening of his door.

Beside her silhouette, another, half her height,
comes forward, inside his cabin, a child,
who turns its back and drops its shorts,
while the girl behind speaks up.

You want smallie boy?
We get you smallie boy.

The speed
at which the naked Rocky
flies from his bunk.

The roar
of his garbled wording
echoed through the ship.

The flight
of girl and boy
down the deck and off.

Come evening he's back out on top for a smoke.
Watching the sun set behind the skyline of Hong Kong.
The fresh warmth of a breeze to spite the ever-heat
before he goes down for his shift, to a place
just as hot, where air cannot blow.

The puzzle of boats still sat out on the water,
homes rippled by the waves that flow beneath.

A girl leaning out of a window, smoking
as he smokes, she gazes up smiling, her shape
just the same as the next, though his guess
from that look on her face, at her having seen him
not so long before. He calls down

   How much?

just like that
with her answer
as quick

   Fifteen dollar.

He gets her on board. It's permitted.
So long as the ship is at anchor.
If she likes she may stay day and night.
The only restriction he must impose
is that she does not share his food.
She is familiar with this ruling.

She calls herself Natasha; her chosen western name.
She is Taiwanese. Her hair is long and straight and black.
She wears a blouse of white silk, a narrow tube
hanging loose past her hips, pink lotus flowers
embroidered on collar and cuffs,
dark blue mini-skirt beneath, reaching little further
than the hem of her white silk blouse;
green-thonged flip-flops adorn her child-like feet.

On his own a while later,
up for a breather,
taking refreshment at Neptune's
when a retired commander sidles down the bar;
in full gold-trimmed uniform,
complete with waxed black moustache.

How are you finding your lobster?

And Rocky's confusion, not just
at the man's half-wink, which could
be merely a twitch, more so
at the fact he only ordered lemonade,
at how the commander isn't eating either,
but halfway through his third double-scotch.

I call mine lobsters, you know.
That way they can go on expenses.
A not-unreasonable luxury.

At which the younger man begins to understand.

Dropped in the pan while alive, so I'm told.
The best way to cook 'em.
Ensures the flesh is tender, is fresh.

At which he's lost him again,
with no opportunity for explanation,
as the man and his moustache
slide back to their end of the bar.

In his cabin, Natasha
has hung out his washing
on sagged lengths of string,
moistening the air with scented soap.

Behind layers of damp swaying cloth
she has emptied his jar of loose change
onto the ironing board,
has separated out the currencies,
stacked the coins and written
her calculations on an envelope.

Twelve dollar.

She looks up, triumphant. She stands.

At current exchange rates.

She puts her arms about his neck.

Today I will show you all of Hong Kong.

They don't go alone.
The second engineer joins them.
He brings his own lobster.
He whispers to Rocky.

> *You can do what you want in this town.*
> *So long as you pay for it.*

They end up doing very little.
Travelling by rickshaws, two apiece,
trotting down many cramped streets
without really going anywhere.

Bored by the leisurely pace, they race,
with this particular two-stroke engine
encouraged to go faster by the frantic
application of more money;
requiring great skill to lean forward
precariously out of the joggling cab,
to wave notes beside the driver's ear,
to negotiate promises in Mandarin,
to increase the flap of his feet.

Resting in the downstairs restaurant
of a recommended brothel-house,
amidst paper lanterns and bamboo,
Rocky stares at the wrong menu,
till Natasha fishes it from his hands
with her chopsticks, passing him instead
the one printed in his own language,
which he closes and puts to one side.

You order on my behalf.
Whatever you give me, I'll eat.

After four days
the hook is lifted;
all girls must leave.

Natasha is crying,
drying her eyes with her hair,
for Rocky has given her
all the loose change from his jar,
transferred to a silk-lined purse
he bought specially at a market stall.

She thanks him.
She kisses him with wet lips.
She thanks him again.
He tells her not to.

It's only a bit of old change.
It would otherwise sit in the cabin unused.
Much better with you than with me.

As the engines are re-started
so Rocky too, disembarks,
the end of his stay in Hong Kong to mark
the end of his six-month stint on board,
leaving as the new crewmen arrive.

He is given an open ticket.
Valid for all military flights.
To take him home,
or anywhere else.

Two big men in padded black leather,
sat at a picnic table, beneath a wide red parasol,
no cloud within the circle of mountain surrounding.

   You thought you could read Chinese,
   just by looking, at first glance.

Two big bikes, balanced side by side in the empty carpark;
their thick rear tyres cushioned to the gravel.
The sun cold on their chrome.

   Not read, not comprehend meaning;
   make sense of; the patterns; they seemed to fit.

The remnants of breakfast. The rind
from three well-done slices of black-pudding.
Smears of egg yolk. Empty cups on small white saucers.

   All these places you go; is it so dull in Scotland?
   what you must think of us stick-in-the-muds.

The thickness of his finger,
pressing the crumbs from the plate,
rubbed by his thumb to fall at his feet.

   It's not the life I set out for; just doing my job;
   these moments, places, just happen on the way.

The other man, shrugging. He stands.
He is taller. He has long blond hair.
He goes off to order more coffee. Comes back.

Okay then; so where did you go after that?
to Peru? the Antarctic? round Russia?

His friend. Gazing down at a fluffed cappuccino.
The dusting of chocolate on foam.
The chip on the rim of the cup swivelled round.

Not much to say about that; these things
aren't important; drink up, we should get on.

Readying herself for the evening shift at the diner. Her blue/
white uniform. Small black shoes. Yellow overcoat.

Still waiting on at fifty. Still happy with her looks. Her
make-up reduced to faint eyeliner, a little lipstick.

At her table: a group of twelve sailors, fresh from their ship.
Except she is told they're not sailors but engineers.

The one they call Rocky orders in French, not too badly.
She asks if he's actually visited France. He has. Just the
once.

Many of the group have girls sat beside them. The girls are
by no means young. Not when compared to the men.

She is asked when her shift finishes. Soon enough. Loitering
contemplatively in the kitchen with their readied plates.

It's Rocky who asks her to join them. He's very polite. He
  stands. Holds her hand in his. Offers a personal tour of
  the ship.

A minor readjustment in the restroom. Re-fixing her hair.
  Unknotting her apron strings. Scrutinizing her figure in
  profile.

They find a new venue. She feels up for anything tonight,
  though perhaps a few drinks may help her along the way.
  They are duly provided.

Leaving the known space of her town, the ship doesn't move
  when she steps aboard, accommodates her weight into its
  world.

Her shiver at the touch of this man, his toughened hands
  removing her uniform. The cold of the floor against her
  naked feet.

He lingers, nearly misses the start of his shift; so Jojo in
  his stead escorts her off-ship; linking arms to steady her
  wobbled step.

She enquires if she was the oldest, of whether Rocky won
  the wager they'd set. Nowhere close. One man came back
  with a lady of sixty-five.

Apologies as she hops to dry land. She doesn't mind, so long
  as she had a pleasant night, with Rocky, quite the best
  part.

He should be resting up with a leg like that.
Instead he moseys down here looking for work.

The disgruntled huff of his Bantam turned off.
Free-wheeling to a stop at the workshop door.
His fake-leather jacket, affording him less
protection than the thickness of jumper beneath.
Swinging out the stiff white log of his cast,
settling the rucked-up hem of his kilt.
A lop-sided crutchless hobble into the office.

No use in restarting his apprenticeship.
Set him to work at once on whatever needs doing.

Syruping the belts slung from the ceiling,
a thick molasses mix painted onto the rubber,
partly soaked in, slowing their slip round the pulleys.

We've a new man, fully qualified; certified.
Just lacks confidence, just needs a few pointers.

Working the milling machine
while the other man watches;
his smooth completion of the task,
holding out the finished metalwork;
the other man turning it over in his hands,
asking to see the process one more time.

He's begun a course at the college. Evening classes.
The work is beneath him, I doubt he'll see it through.

A simple exercise for which
he does not have the necessary tool,
so he goes to the tool-station,
manufactures the implement needed,
returns to his workbench, gets on.

Some students like his help, the way he explains things.
Others don't like him at all, just being there.

Making his slow way out of the college grounds.
Keeping to the grass beside the path to soften his limp.
Two teenaged slackers creeping through the dark.
Catching hold of one in their failed attack, a few
stiff punches to the gut, ensures they won't try again.

Unfathomable, why it's him gets singled out.
Though no man is ever free of idiots.

Dragging the keel up the Yellow River.

From within, a new frequency to fill the gaps between
the hammering of engine noise, an unrelenting gentle hiss,
as liquid-crystal sediments of silt caress the hull.

From without, a crust of barnacles gathered from the sea,
now dying in this wash of inland water, jellied bodies
bursting in their home-spun shells, picked clean away.

Pulling up outside Puyang,
glimpses of the boat below the waterline
are silver, the grey paint stripped,
the metal polished, smooth as mercury.

The crew lined up on deck to receive their host;
each man presented with his own Red Guard,
his personal protector, with rifle and holstered gun,
to go wherever he may go, in order to learn English.

Each guard to give their charge a copy
of Mao's LITTLE RED BOOK, in stylish plastic covers
blocked in gold, in hope the great departed will continue
to inspire; the shock of loss still wavered through their land.

Stationed just outside his cabin door, it's
not easy to relax, so Rocky invites his in
with calming gestures, his duty
to teach the man as best he can.

  Oakaedeno
  Ouk oi danu
  Orc hai tonoh
  Och aye the noo

Picking through the semi-see-through pages
of Mao's quotes as he lies on his bunk,
trying to match the lines of Cantonese
on one page with the English on the next.
Partial recognition, the sense he used to know
these word-shapes, long ago, now wholly forgotten.

His protector, hunched upon the cradle
of the daybed, the upturned half-moon,
studying with care the pages of a dirty magazine.
The look on his small round face, a child-like awe,
stiffening at every noise, sharp glances at the door.

Signs and smiles convey that he may keep the magazine,
and the guard's struggle to recall the word for thanks
imparts his gratitude more perfectly than words,
as Rocky chaperones him to the bathroom down the hall,
nipping back for his own five minutes alone.

Little more than a pit-stop,
a tip-toe testing of the waters;
with the trial visit over,
the guards are marched off,
and the boat departs.

Weeds holding fast to the hull.
Long green watery ribbons of algae
streaming through the yellow water,
rooted in unseen scratches
left by the silt.

When the ship reaches ocean
the weeds fall away.

She's out at a disco with friends, the girl
he'll someday fall in love with;
not yet, not tonight.

She's got all the get-up,
the ultra-short skirt, the black stockings,
the boots she once dared to spray silver,
the sequins she sewed down the seams
of her favourite creamy-white blouse.

She has curled out the hang of her bobbed black hair.
Her lipstick is pink. Her eye-shadow blue.
Beneath all this she's a hospital nurse.
Not tonight.

She's no dolly.
She likes to think she's prettier than that.
Though sometimes it's more fun to cover it up.

And it's fine, for a while, she fits in.
Does a good job of spinning about with the rest.
Of shouting to be heard above the din.

Till he arrives. Floating onto the dance floor.
Full Highland regalia: knee-length socks,
tasselled garters, black brogues, tweedy jacket, the lot.
As though he's come straight from a wedding;
perhaps not.

He dances Strathspeys
to a disco pulse;
a Reel for new wave rock;
the DJ tries funk,
he opts for Gay Gordon.

The crowd cheer him on, for a while.
He seems to enjoy it. The nurse, her mouth,
indecisive, smiles one moment, flattened the next.

And when he begins to look for partners
encouraging others to join him,
they don't want to know,
it's not what they're here for.

He singles her out, because she just stands there,
because she was slow catching on to the change in mood.

Half a dance with him and she's breathless.
The novelty of his appearance has gone.
He gives it a rest, escorts her to the edge of the hall.

They sit side by side.
She drinks water. He chats.
But the music is too loud.
She points to her ear and shrugs.
He leads her outside.
She doesn't resist.

The streets are deserted.
The night wind is icy.
He suggests coffee.
She agrees though cannot think where.

His wood-framed Morris estate parked near by.
And soon the internal heater is blowing
warm air around her ankles, her knees,
whilst the city flows by and behind them.

He talks about engines.
She talks about nursing.
He says how he's never quite free
from the blackening oils.
She says how most of her patients
stink of alcohol and piss.

She asks what he gets up to on his travels.
He says he must concentrate on driving.
This part of the road is un-made.
No street-light to mark the soft verges.

The grass has begun to dew.
It is long. She lifts her silver boots high
not to get her stockings damp.

It is quiet in the park.
The other caravans are asleep,
huge rectangular beasts kneeling
awkwardly upright in the field.

The city, compacted by distance,
a dome of loosed light glowing yellow
its corner of sky.

His home is larger, is warmer, inside
than its dulled white shell might suggest.

He makes coffee. She flops to the couch.
Too late now for music. She's hungry.
A packet of biscuits is opened.
She watches him closely. He fidgets.

Once when in China they went to the theatre.
A long red carpet laid out, though they
walked beside it, not knowing.
And the play made no sense,
very slow, with elaborate dresses,
and candles, and slow-motion swordplay,
and thin whiney music, all wavering voices,
and high chiming cymbals, and flowers.

Her eyes are insistent, though drooping
they won't let him go, and he squirms to tell more.

One time the argon pipe sheared on the fridges.
The meat, the vegetables, all went rotten,
had to be thrown overboard.
For days they ate nothing but cheese.
Even now finds it hard to stomach the smell
of even the mildest of cheddars.

That's not it. She knows. He knows.
Still tentatively he continues.

Everyone in grey suits, like pyjamas,
and matching grey caps to cover their hair.
Coats buttoned up to the neck.
The women with chests strapped flat.
The men no bigger than their counterparts.

Not much interested in politics,
nor even in his doings on the boat.

He breathes out.
He tells her.
Admitting his shame.
That he can't write.
That he can't even read.

She glances away.
Her eyelids are heavy.
She never wanted to be a nurse.
Hoped one day to be a scientist.
Yet here she is nursing.
Albeit not tonight.

Falling asleep where she lies.
He does not try to move her.
Plenty of blankets to cover her up.
Removes her dangled coffee cup.

Grass grown up around his caravan.
Grass through the spokes of his Bantam.
He's out cutting it when she awakes.
Adjusting the mower's undulating note.

When he comes in she's at the table.
She has laid out paper and pens.
God knows where she found them.
She's drawing single letters on each page.
Big beautifully elegant shapes.
Magnifying her natural hand.

She shows him the pages.
He wants to make breakfast.
She pleads with him to try.

Not just their meanings he forgot.
The problem goes deeper than that.

She asks he do just one.
One letter. The first in his name.
Sits him down.
Gives him the page to copy.

The stutter of his hand
to move pen over paper
to repeat the simple curl,
the concentration on his face
for this one giant squiggle.

She stops him.
Laying her hand over his
to finish the shape.

The tip of the welding rod
melting itself to the gap
between railing and deck,
shortening its stiffness
into quick liquidity.

The stub discarded
he feels behind
for another, from a box
no longer there.

Karachi

They are here to re-stock the ship.
Fresh fuel. Fresh water. Fresh food,
to be swapped with what's left of the cheese.

They are here to salvage a Rolls-Royce turbine
from one of their derelict vessels,
peeling back the thick metallic skin,
reaching in, to hook the innards up and out.

Hazy grey dawn above the shore's yellow dust
as a derrick ratchets the precision machinery
into air and over water; dangled open-ended pipes
swaying as the block is angled round,
till the crane's operator misjudges the height
and takes out the rails of the ship,
plucked from the deck-edge,
bending as easy as string to trail from the turbine,
to drag long bright scratches through the paintwork
as the spoil comes to rest on the foc'sle.

Out on the make-shift harbour: a high-wire fence
erected to keep out the locals;
still they somehow manage to get in,
slotting each other like toy blocks through portholes,
taking pencils, letters, fiction, odd socks, anything;
patted down if discovered, few items, if any, returned.

Rocky, kneeling on his rubber mat,
the deep magenta lenses of his goggles
flashing pink the welding arc that sprouts from his hands.

Sweat on his forearms, sweat in his hair,
kept by the seal of the goggles from flooding his eyes.
Working fast to fit the semi-straightened railings back in place,
or maybe they would try to take those too.

His box had been near empty.
A few long grey needles loose within the cardboard.
No footsteps over the crackle of his work.
No hollow rattle as the box was snatched.
Sneaking. Shadowless. Silent. Gone.

His gear, packed away for the sake of fetching
a few more rods, carried with him below decks.
Glimpsing as he goes: a fleeing brown-skinned leg;
a hand groping under a door, hastily withdrawn;
the shine of white eyes and white teeth, receding into shadow.
Like an infestation of ants, never congregating where
the poison's at; or a rat, that scarpers at his booted approach.

Till by chance he spies two, busy behind a bulkhead,
in sandals and shirts, naked in between,
one thin-limbed and small, one muscular and tall,
the former being buggered by the latter, unprotesting.

So Rocky, lowering his pack,
unhooks the fire extinguisher from the wall,
pulls the pin, points the nozzle, and squeezes.

The sting of the water jet sends them howling
up and out and off the ship,
leaving their shorts behind.

An officer,
having witnessed the high-pressure dousing,
draws Rocky aside, through clenched teeth
reminds him that he's not here to interfere,
that what the locals do amongst themselves
is not for him to judge; leaning closer to whisper
an extra few words, that should he chance to see,
floating with the oils, the plastic wrap, the muck,
anything resembling a body, to think of it
as driftwood, as seaweed, and pay it no mind.

Finishing work on the railings,
one arm looped through his tool-bag,
he heads for the flat of the prow,
from his bag lifts an old pair of boots.

Steel toe-capped, steel heeled.
The inner soles worn through.
Unwearable. Fit for the bin.
He sets them neatly.
Ties their laces in a bow.
Then welds them, fore and aft,
onto the sun-bright metal of the deck.

Nipping to the midship tower he points to the doubled speck.
Suggests they keep a tally as he goes to resume his shift.

One o'clock in the afternoon.
The hottest quietest hour of the day.
A stillness waiting only to be pricked.

Fingers over the rim of the boat.
A black head slick with oily water.
A framework of limbs holding position,
tangled round the railings.

Hands slipped under rubber arches,
buckling the worn-out leather,
tugging the combined ship-mass,
till a blast from the speakers,
a trumpet, a commanding voice,
followed by the body-streak,
the unchecked leap, the pause
before the splash.

Some minutes go by,
the head reappears,
is bolder; this time
when it flees the boots
sit laceless in the sun.

But the man in the tower cannot see
in all directions, has other duties to perform;
his attention brought back by rapid
high-pitched tappings,
their distance, insistence,
sees a figure sitting,
wrapped about the boots,
protectively cross-legged,
holding chisel-tip
to the bridge of molten metal,
wooden mallet fraying at the edges
where it strikes its mark.

The body once more scared away,
soon returns,
its actions muffled this time by a rag,
still punctuate their note within the tower;
newly fleeing,
newly coming back,
the play goes on.

Till the look-out tires of his role.
Till one by one the welds are broken.

And, one by one,
the boots are snaffled,
body-hugged,
transported off the ship,
beyond its bounds,
beyond caring.

The gaffer in his MG Midget.
His white-skinned rag-topped gem;
albino dragonfly, newly buzzing from its nymphal skin.
He's had it for three weeks. Still new.

Rolling smoothly over courtyard cobbles.
Deep-tread tyres sucking to the gaps
as to the polished stone.

He leaves it running, whilst he idles
in its cramped two-seater cockpit
filing streetmaps in the tight
elasticated pockets of its doll's-house doors,
a tin of humbugs slotted beneath the dash,
the engine twisted off as if in afterthought.

Flipping the keys as he strolls to his office
once about their ring to rest in his palm,
he passes Rocky lingering half-out of the workshop,
wiping his fingers on a cloth as he frowns
towards the tick of the slowly cooling car

I'll take a look at it, if you'd like.
It's new, Rocky.
The engine needs tuning.
Rocky, it's new.
It's only out a touch, it won't take long.
Sounded fine to me.
I heard it different.

so hands him the key.

Four guys. Four girls.
Meeting at a pub on the corner of Leith.
Just a gathering point before they head off
to a ceilidh some miles out of town.

Three pairs already half-filled with beer,
loping heavy down the road,
following Rocky into a sidestreet
pausing as he unlocks a small white car.

Where's the woody at?
In bits on my lawn.
We can't all fit in this.
No, you can't.

As he eases in one side,
the nurse in the other.

No problem, we'll wait; come fetch us in turn.
You know, it's six miles out to Musselburgh.
Aye, we know, but we've still got to get there.
And six of you; not such a difficult sum.

As the ignition fires on a whisper,
a buzz of wings beneath the bonnet;
a tightness of compacted muscle
set against the lightness of its frame.

In this thing it won't take you long.
On that I agree.
And you can't go leaving folk behind.
Maybe, sometimes, that's best.

As an eagerness of wheels rolls the tarmac
out behind them, as its hum gets higher,
flashing its pallid flank as it turns and is gone.

Captain and Chief
out for a stroll on the deck,
hands clasped behind them,
surveying the seascape.

There's a problem with my fourth engineer.
I heard it was with your fifth.
You mean Rockcliffe?
Is that not more likely?
I don't think so.

The skin of water opened wide,
a cut, forced apart by the bow
digging a ship-shaped trench
through flesh closed up behind.

I heard Rockcliffe was slack in his duties.
That is the complaint being made.
Not making water, not checking the oil.
That is what the fourth has been saying.
And what of Rockcliffe's defence?
I've not seen the need to speak to him yet.

Rocky, beginning his shift,
greeted by the chirping of alarms,
a spray of red blinking lights;
works his way through till they stop.

I've conducted my investigation.
Without speaking to the one concerned?
The logbooks are witness enough.
I thought Rockcliffe doesn't like to write.
A painful hand to read, but concise.
The entries could be falsified.
I dipped the tanks, it's his accounts that tally.

Pumping the bilge oil through.
Making gas seals for compressors;
not part of his duty, just bored;
seeking out further odd jobs to do.

A bit fishy for Rockcliffe not to complain.
It's not in his nature to make a fuss.
You mean because he's the junior rank?
Not just that, and anyway, not for much longer.

The fourth, sat in the control room,
writing lengthy letters home,
chewing the cap of his pen,
while the gauges twitch into red.

I hinted demotional notions to the fourth.
I take it he wasn't enthused at the prospect.
I suggested Mr Rockcliffe take his place.
A straight swap seems only fair.
He swore that Rockcliffe was the one to blame.
The truth will out; there being only one.
He knew it; now he knows the reason why.

The Chief, propped against the railings,
sea-spit on his face, salt winds
thickening his hair. The Captain,
laughing, spinning his cap on the air.

A lightweight package through her letterbox.
A bulky envelope with foreign stamps.
A scratch of paper flopping to the mat.

Enough to rouse her,
to have her downstairs in her gown;
more delight in this moment of anticipation,
the scooping up of all the mail,
the leaving of his till last.

The nurse
at her breakfast,
her sweetened tea,
her marmalade on toast,
yellow sunlight through net curtains,
loose pages spread over the table.

He is in British Columbia.
The cold is getting to his leg.
He is having fun with explosives.

The nurse
coming in from her nightshift,
knocking snow from her boots,
removes her heavy overcoat.

Stoking the wood-burning stove,
a sheaf of papers in her other hand,
his word-shapes only recognisable
because she taught him how to make them;
her easy decoding of his phonetical style.

Now passing through Melanesia.
They have a local drink he's partial to.
A peaceful paradisal sort of place.

The nurse
in her bath,
putting paper between her eyeline
and the naked white bulb overhead.

The damp of her skin
absorbed by the letter.
Ink-stains on fingers.
Dust from a frayed envelope
flecking the wet of her hair.

Gone walkabout in the Antipodes.
A way of life that suits him to a tee.
Can't say for sure when he'll be coming back.

The paper gone floppy from steam.

She places it outside the tub,
on a stool beside her leafy gold watch,
beside her wedding ring,
its stone of oceanic blue.
Slides herself forward and down.

The rub of her back on the warm white ceramic.
The slop and suck of water closed over her head.

Black sky above the Western Pacific rim.
Black sea hushing round the shallow rocks.

A blacked-out ship; one more island in the archipelago.
Nine black diamonds, hollowed, cresting the wavelets.

Elongated tight-skinned prows, parting reeds.
Sunk in fresh water, weighted to the silt with stones.

Figures moving inland through fields of sugar cane.
Warm winds to lift the moisture from their guns.

The one with the limp, so slick over water, now dealing
with the fence, neutralising currents, without a spark.

A lone gaoler, woken at the prod of a rifle's muzzle.
A seven-foot minister, unbuckled from his false imprisonment.

Up to the big house on the hill, passing the other team
sleepwalking their immigrant captives down to the cells.

Island Royalty, high government, Eton-educated native folk,
re-inserted doll-like in the roles. Tucked into their postered beds.

The wire, reconnected. Wavered grooves through sugar cane.
Black specks heading out towards the thinly blued horizon.

Two days on, and a ship,
idling through the region,
chooses to drop in on Fiji.

Meetings of host and guest,
ensuring all is well;
invited to stay for a while.

A guided tour of their fields
on a single-gauge track,
a little engine fed on black treacle.

Rocky on a grass sward by the sea,
smoked fish on plates of woven leaves
presented by girls taller than him by a half.

Pimped as local finery, yet free to him
at their own wish, stroking his soft white skin
with long brown fingers.

They prepare fresh kava,
grinding the root with stones,
sieved through a sock into coconut halves.

He sips the thick grey paste.
It tastes of sweetened aniseed.
He knocks it back. They cheer.

Four cups in, he tries to stand, his legs
have rubberised. Their cries
become the sighings of the sea.

The land around him rises, falls,
is breathing as he breathes. Its face
of cocoa sky, its round brown eyes,

her mouth, a narrow wood-carved boat,
skipping over glitter, the ripples of her hair
a sail, its tips to scratch the clouds,

to tickle the bellies of sharks,
backward smiling, pink-lipped
breaching, catching flying fish

by hand, a bed of blue-
green scales, as slippy as silk,
returning full to land.

The dark heat of his cabin as he swings from his bunk.
A low drone cutting through his metalled world.

Six large jam-jars, their insides like cement.
A potency diminished, retreating from its source.

Promoted to third engineer.
Unlikely to go any further.
Not without taking exams.
The price of the officer's ticket.
Wherein the problem lies.

A third is required to write reports.
On generators, valves, core pressure,
cavitation damage, ear-ache.
An initial drawback, till
he is told he may dictate.

Pacing the control room,
no fear of articulation.
The junior bowed at the desk,
scribbling his every spoken word.
Better this way for all concerned.

The Chief in his oak-panelled office.
Snug between antique filing cabinets.
Leafing through the reports.
Praising their conciseness, their detail.
Telling Rocky he could go far.

I recommend you try night school.
Oh, but I couldn't do that, sir.
Clear this little hurdle of yours.
I could never go back, sir.
Be sure to consider the matter.

Dismissed with a lifted left hand.
The Chief, head down, intent
upon his own written work.
The stubborn scratch of pen on paper.
The crooked discipline in every line.

Arrival by night at his cottage
in Fife. To his wife. To the children
asleep in their room opposite.

The black gap of a door left ajar
as he passes by, leaves both children and nurse
undisturbed, to settle his pack in the spare,
where the single bunk is always made up
for guests, for unexpected visitors.

A corner of light in the dark of the house
as he unbuckles from his tired uniform,
leaving the window angled upward a crack,
still partly clothed as he eases under the sheets.

A boy of five.
A girl of three.
Dressed in their weekday best.
Being hurried by their mother
to finish their beakers of juice,
the milk left in their bowls.

Eyeing their father as he comes in,
as he stands with his back to them,
pressing bread into the toaster,
emptying the teapot into his cup.

The radio is on.
Their mother is counting down from ten.
Their father makes faces behind her.
The children don't smile. Wide-eyed.
Small people with small expressions.

Then they are gone.
Driven away at speed.
One to school,
the other to nursery.

When she returns the dishes
are already washed and dried,
the table cleared away.

They'll greet you properly
when they come back.
They usually do.

He is sat in the lounge, turning
the pages of school-books,
his tea gone cold in the cup.

Why not set up as a mechanic.
We've enough to start you up on.
You've served for so many years.
They'd surely let you go at once.

Not looking her way.
Picking a toy motorbike from the floor.
Idly separating out its parts.

Not mechanic. Toolmaker.
The one good bit of advice I got.
To learn to make the things
by which all other things are made.

She sits across from him.
Her hair is shorter than when he saw her last.
Less nurse now, more mother.

Do that then. So long as you leave.
I'm on leave now.
Leave-leave. Properly. Give up. Forever.
I'll be sure to consider the matter.

She lets him alone for a while.
She sees he is tired.
It's only his first day back.

The toy bike in bits before him.
He begins to fit it together again.

Finishing one more stint on water.
Dropped off in Cape Town.

Pay packet in hand.
His open ticket home.
The other men, going off alone.

He heads for the Holiday Inn.
A high room; cheap and clean.
Overlooking Table Bay.

A small grey island four miles out.
Beyond: the slow bright curve
of the world, its everlasting drop.

Come morning he does
what he usually does in new places,
he wanders, he heads to the harbour,
follows his feet towards water.

The day is cold, is sharp with autumn light.
He gets chatting to a black chap at the docks.
They share cigarettes.

Your accent, you're not from round here.
I'm from Scotland.
I don't know that land.
Next to England.
Ah, yes.

Another man arrives.
A white man in a white suit.
White hair beneath his broad-brimmed hat.
He speaks to the black man,
conversing in Afrikaans, while Rocky
listens, saying nothing.

The man owns a small fleet of boats.
Commercial tugs, a cargo ferry.
Squat-bodied vessels, snub-nosed, muscular.
The young Scotsman is given a tour.

One of the tugs is not working.
In a state of abandoned repair.
Its inside exposed to the cold salt air.
Rocky offers to take a look.

  I can't pay you.
  I'm not fussed about that.

Still there when the red sun sets
behind the island across from the bay.
Oil in his hair, on his lips, in his eyes.
Black hand-prints on his borrowed overalls.

Still there when the owner pulls up in his silver Mercedes.
Tells Rocky to leave it, to come for a drive, for a drink.

I don't drink.
Then let me do the drinking.
The work isn't finished.
It's better by far than it was.

A plastic cover fixed to the passenger seat.
Rocky keeps his hands to his lap.
The car rolling noiselessly south out of town,
fast through the dusk along slow curving roads.

No notable decrease in speed as they veer from the main,
heading out to the coast on a single-lane track,
the far-off mumble of grit churned up by the tyres
curling outward into the dark of the fields either side.

Speckles of light up ahead. A high wall.
Passing through an automated gate
yawning at their rapid approach.
Followed by flowers,
a night-lit garden of tropical plants
to border the rise of the driveway.

A house overlooking the ocean,
faced with smoked glass.
Seeming no more than a bungalow,
till he learns how its front
cuts down into the cliff-face,
levelling into a short plateau,
before a last drop to the water.

   My daughter. Alexis.

A girl of nineteen,
sat out on the veranda,
a book in one hand,
cigarette in the other,
not much of her in between,
standing to greet him, very tall,
wide-mouthed, long brown hair,
little tits,

    It's Alex, if you wouldn't mind.

as her grip
lingers after his own is relaxed,
her fingers dragged over his palm.

After dinner, her father
drinks himself into a doze,
is left in his chair,
while the girl
leads their guest to her room.

Come morning he is seen
only by the old black gardener,
who pauses in his work,
straightens to watch the young man
strolling through the day's early wetness.

Unable to rouse the automated gate,
he shins up and over the wall,
as the gardener bends back to his tending.

Half a mile to the main road.
Thirty more thumbed from a pick-up.
First to the hotel, to check out,
transferring his gear to the docks,
to a place called The Seaman's Cabin,
before heading down to the tugs,
to continue with his repairs.

The black fellow
helping him out with his work,
bringing cartons of tea for them both,
the silence of their break, broken,
as Rocky watches a small boat
chug out towards the island.

>   *What is it they keep out there?*
>   *Political prisoners; don't get me started.*
>   *Maybe someone should mount an escape.*
>   *It's our boat they use to ferry supplies.*
>   *Lots of things could be snuck aboard a boat like that.*
>   *Lots of hiding places.*

They finish their tea.
They get back to work.

Alex arrives at midday.
She waits for Rocky to clean himself up,
then takes him to a seafood restaurant.
She has grilled abalone with okra.
He has prawns.

They drive north through the mountains. Her car:
a third series Lotus Esprit, in lilac.
Roof-mounted speakers. Scarlet upholstery.

Jazz re-workings of the Brandenburgs
pour loud around them. She hums along,
sitting slightly forward in her seat,
wearing large dark glasses,
her bare arms parallel and straight,
long fingers curled tight round the red leather wheel,
her honeysuckle scents hovering
in the stuffy closed-in space.

She moves the car at speed. With precision.
Flowing it smoothly round dawdlers,
blinking her tail as she rockets ahead.
Never slowing for corners,
her trust in the car
to keep itself stuck to the road.

She brakes only once
when a big baboon struts
on all fours sedately
across the road ahead,
calmly glancing their way
as they close in upon it.

A sharp squeak from her,
the car's dutiful drop in pace,
as the ape disappears,
as the speed is resumed,
with her sighing angrily
back to her upright alertness.

I hate them.
You saw how he looked at me.
Looked right at me.
As though he had as much right.
It gives me the creeps.

Whilst Rocky just braces,
his fist round the door-hold,
in fear of his prawns reappearing.

A valley of tall yellow grasses
between round-topped mountains.
The pallid Lotus parked
beneath a red-leafed tree.

Alex, leaning in to the back seat,
passing out a long black rifle,
followed by one for herself.

> *You don't have to shoot it if you don't want to.*
> *So long as you keep a lookout for things stalking me.*

She has on hiking boots, blue denim shorts.
Her hair in two long pigtails down her back.
The brim of her white canvas hat
flopped forward over her eyes.
Beneath a green-checked sleeveless shirt
the thin yellow straps of her needless bra,
forever slipping loose about her arms.

One shot is all she manages.
A loud clear crack
repeats round the mountains
and off down the valley,
over the heads of the springbok
who scatter, unhurt,
as she lowers the weight of the gun
to the soft mossy ridge
on which they both lie,
as he removes his squint
from his field-glasses,
glancing at the empty sky.

Not much will want to stray this way for a while.

Scanning again for the herd,

Though there's always a chance.

as Alex rolls onto her back
to unzip her shorts.

A visit from her father at the docks,
where Rocky, finished with one boat,
has begun on another.

You're a good man to have around.
You're resourceful. Not a slacker.

Treating him to lunch.
A swordfish steak for himself.
Rocky opting for salad.

The girl likes you. I like you.
If you want to marry her, please,
we would all be very happy.

And as they part
the man in his big white suit and hat
hands Rocky a thin pig-skin wallet.
Not much to look at,
heavier than it looks.

Back in his quarters he unwraps the wallet,
tips six small gold coins into his palm.
Each no larger than a new English penny,
but thinner, and brighter, and rounder.
Packed deep with the rest of his gear.

At the military airport
a secretary calculates the quickest way
to get him home again,
writing down the points of change,
and handing him the slip,
which he looks at for a long time,
then glances back up.

   What other destinations do you have?

The attic of a neighbouring cottage.
Fitting new pipework following a thaw.
The neighbour sat at the base of wooden steps,
his back to the square black hole they extend from.

The quality of paint applied is irrelevant.
The manner of application secondary to the depiction.

Rocky, finishing up, his tools put away,
lights off, listening to the intermittent knocking overhead.

Yet the form employed defines the image.
The paint whether cheap or dear becomes the painting.

Acorns, like slow hard rain, sudden windfall,
striking the corrugated sheeting of the roof.
He lifts a hatch, pokes his head into hot dry air.

The yellow brightness of the Suez Canal,
its calm blue band of water eddying by,
whorls on its flattish surface silver the sun.

Distant figures cresting the pale bank of sand.
Arabs made triangular by a splay of headdress and robe.
Little puffs of cordite smoke, fast followed
by the ping and bounce of the bullet striking the hull,
the muffled rifle-pop to come after.

Rocky, lowering the hatch,
securing himself back into the dark,
to the slow tap of acorns
dropped onto the roof.

The care put to each brushstroke un-witnessed.
As means should not dictate the choosing of paints.

Coming down through the square black hole.
The neighbour pausing his monologue
to help him collapse the stairway.
Standing on tip-toes to shut the trap-door.

How about if we move to Australia.
And the children?
We'll take them too.
I mean their schooling.
They have schools in Australia.
What of my family? My friends?
They're half the reason for going.
And my job? And yours?
It's a big place; plenty of work.
We're just getting settled.
Maybe you are; maybe that's the trouble.
You want us to move to the ends of the earth.
It's not how they see it themselves.
Just pack up the house and go. I don't think so.
It'll be an adventure.
No, Rocky, not with what I have to deal with here.
Exactly, forget all that, leave it behind.
I'll have to deal with the same and worse when there.
Not at all, it's fairly easy living.
With poisonous spiders, and snakes, and dry dust.
Far stranger animals than that, but they won't harm you.
I don't know what that means, but no thank you.
Come on, it needn't be forever, a few years.
No, Rocky.
A couple of months, an extended holiday.
Rocky, no.

He is quiet after that
making no further mention.
Quiet all evening, over dinner,
lying still the whole night through.

And come morning
when they are away,
he packs a small bag
with essentials, not much:
his passport, his wallet,
a toy car, his kilt.

Then he goes out,
down the lane, over fields,
to the bus stop, requests
a ticket, one-way,
for the end of the line.

You awake to nothing,
to nowhere, deprived
of your senses, alone
in darkness, but floating.

An empty vessel,
deserted, you go
to the noticeboard, seeing
where you've turned out.

A pinned streetmap,
monotoned, flat,
names you recognise,
in all the wrong places.

Princes and George
joined end to end.
Leith Walk shorter
than you remember.

Waverly too far out.
Saint Kilda too far in.
Roslyn, Corstorphine,
Musselburgh, Canongate.

Mixed with others
you know, and don't.
Not that it matters
what's in a name.

This is Dunedin,
New Zealand,
Edinburgh of the South.
It'll do well enough.

Where you'll stay
for a while, or longer;
a home, and half the world
away from home.

Ⓑ editions